The Story of Snowy Bear and the Lost Scarf

· Co-Authors ·

TC LiFonti

Charles "Peanut" Tillman

· Illustrator ·

Gabrielle Esposito

MW01251504

Charles Tillman
CORNERSTONE 33
FOUNDATION

www.charlestillman.org

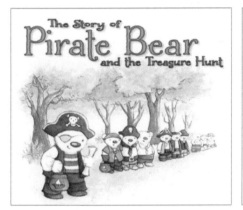

All book titles benefit the Charles Tillman Cornerstone Foundation.

ISBN-13: 978-0692352014
ISBN-10: 0692352015

Special thanks to Karen Hahn for the art creation of Snowy Bear, Paul Faris as Art Director, and to Amelia Burford, Editor.

One morning Snowy Bear woke up
and saw that it was snowing!

Quickly, he ran downstairs...

...to ask Mama Bear...

...if he could go
outside and play.

"Mama Bear, Mama Bear!" Snowy Bear said.
"May I please go outside and play?"

"Of course you can go outside, honey," Mama
Bear said. "But you have to make sure that
you dress warm. And don't forget..."

...but before Mama Bear could finish, Snowy was running upstairs yelling, "Thank you, Mama Bear, I'm going to get dressed right now!"

The first thing Snowy Bear did was put on his snowy pants and snowy socks.

Then he put on his favorite snowy sweater.

Finally, he put on his snowy
boots, his snowy jacket,
his snowy hat, and his
snowy gloves...

...but Snowy Bear could not find his snowy scarf.

Quickly, Snowy rushed to his closet and pulled everything out...

...but he did not find his snowy scarf there.

Next, he looked under his bed.

But all he found was his football, his toy truck,
and his toy soldier.

Still searching, he went through his drawers tossing everything out...

...but he could not find his snowy scarf anywhere.

Sadly, he took off his snowy hat, snowy gloves, and snowy jacket.

Then he took off his snowy boots and snowy sweater...

...and finally, he took off his snowy pants and snowy socks.

Mama Bear heard the crying and peeked in.
"Snowy, honey, why are you crying?"

Snowy sniffled, "I cannot find my snowy scarf. And I cannot go out and play without it."

Mama Bear shook her head, "Snowy, honey, don't you remember the snowy snowman you made yesterday with Papa Bear?"

Slowly, Snowy went to the window where he saw the snow falling on his snowman...

...and his blue snowy scarf waving in the wind.

"Mama Bear, Mama Bear!" Snowy exclaimed.
"Look! Look at my snowman!"

"There's my scarf! There it is!
It's right where I left it!"

"That's right, honey," Mama Bear said.
"Don't you remember putting your scarf on
him last night to keep him warm?"

"Yes, Mama Bear, I remember now."

And suddenly Snowy Bear was happy again.

Mama Bear smiled,
"Now get dressed, honey. It's cold outside."

And soon, Snowy Bear was outside in his
snowy scarf playing in the snow.

The End.

SONYA MARTIN PHOTOGRAPHY

The mission of the Charles Tillman Cornerstone Foundation is to provide opportunities and resources to children and their families who are in need.

. . .

A percentage of each book sold will directly benefit the foundation and its efforts to continually help those needing assistance.

Charles Tillman
CORNERSTONE
33
FOUNDATION

www.charlestillman.org

Charles Locker · This program enriches the lives of chronically and critically ill children by providing them and their families with access to iPads, notebook computers, DVD players, portable Play Station game systems, and other electronic handheld games, to pass the time during recovery and treatment.

Field of Dreams · A program that provides chronically and critically ill children and their families with magical memories by fulfilling sports-related wishes. Throughout the year, we offer unique opportunities including tickets to Bears games.

Holiday Celebration · In December, Charles, his wife, Jackie, and a few of Santa's elves visit Chicago-area hospitals to pass out gifts, visit with families and partake in hospital activities, like bingo, to help spread holiday cheer.

TendHER Heart Luncheon · Each spring more than 150 mothers of critically and chronically ill children are invited to attend a special brunch, honoring them for the sacrifices they make in caring for their ill child. The brunch will provide these women with the opportunity to "take a minute" for themselves and enjoy each other's company and support.

Tiana Fund · The Tiana Fund program provides assistance to economically at-risk persons or families in-need that will strengthen their ability to care for themselves, enhance their stability and security, and improve their quality of life or their ability to contribute to the community. Applications are only available at Chicago-area hospitals or pre-approved community organizations.

Made in the USA
Monee, IL
09 December 2020